"Gee, i Wish i Had Been Drinking at the Time"

101
Real Reasons
Why You Never
Hear Those Words

Bill Belew
illustrations by S. Akeala

Copyright © 2007, 2008 by William C. Belew

All rights reserved, including the right to reproduce this work in any form whatsoever without permission in writing from the publisher.

For information or inquiries, write to:

Do Good Books Publishing Company
(a division of Do Good Music)
2134 Edgewood Dr.
Palo Alto, CA 94303

E-mail: 101@dogoodbooks.com
Web: http://www.dogoodbooks.com

Phone: 650-858-1324
Fax: 650-618-1402

This book was designed using Adobe® InDesign® on Apple® Macintosh computers. The primary fonts used are Adobe Garamond Pro and Funhouse.

Interior design by Lewis Greer. Cover design and illustrations by S. Akeala.

ISBN 0-9712723-5-2

Published by Do Good Books

10 9 8 7 6 5 4 3 2

CONTENTS

LAUGHERS   11
Naked sleepwalkers, fake lawyers, legless man, screwing a goat and stuck in a chimney....

SHAKERS   33
Love triangles, repossessed children, drunken pilots, Wal-mart binge, nude students....

MOANERS   55
Strip clubs, being undressed, sexual harassment, $53,000 parties....

GROANERS   77
Stripper poles, month long hangovers, 3-day binges, naked on a freeway, sex with a sidewalk....

DESTROYERS   99
Picking up an 84-year old, being stuck for drinks, losing babies, 20 years in prison, grim reaper, kill or be raped....

PREFACE

It's a good thing nobody knew about alcohol poisoning and that it could kill people back in the '70s. Chances are I wouldn't have lived to put this little toilet reader together.

Friends of mine and I were hanging out at Shakey's Pizza after a basketball game. Somebody smuggled a pint of 86 proof whiskey into the place. I don't remember the brand of the whiskey, I'm lucky I remember this much.

I took a swig. My friend took a swig. I guzzled the rest in about 3-4 seconds. The next thing I remember was waking up in the hospital with a lump on my head and feeling broken.

My friend, Barney, laughed, "Fred, it's no wonder your head hurts so bad. When you tried to walk up to the stage to sing, you caught your foot on one of those short stools and went down. You didn't even put your hands out to break your fall. You landed smack on your forehead."

I was just 17 years old at the time.

Another story –

A policeman found a fellow found wobbling down the street. He wasn't causing anyone any harm. He just looked lost and confused. The policeman decided to give him a lift home. After all, it was well after midnight.

"Yesh, officer. Thash my street."

The officer drove slowly.

"Yesh, officer. Thash my house."

The officer stopped.

The man fell out of the car and landed near the sidewalk.

The cop thought he might as well walk him up to the house.

"Yesh, officer. Thash my front door."

It opened by itself.

"Thash the staircase leading to my bedroom."

The officer sighed and walked him up the stairs.

"Thash my bedroom officer."

The policeman worried that the missus was going to come out any minute.

The two looked into the bedroom and the drunk said, "And, look officer, thash me in bed wiff my wife."

Not funny. Funny.

The first story about me is true. The second isn't about me and it's not true. And, if it were true, it wouldn't be funny when the guy sobered up, would it?

The mini-stories the reader will find in this toilet reader are all true and verified.

So, why did I put this reader together?

I'd like to save that till the end.

For now, have a seat, gather your friends around and have a read.

Bill Belew

For Lennie and Della

INTRODUCTION

Laughers, Shakers, Moaners, Groaners and Destroyers—these are the sub-headings of the five sections.

A drunk can be pretty fun to watch when he or she is not hurting themselves or anyone else they love.

Imagine a guy trying to ride a bicycle with no front wheel, for example, but too drunk to know.

I'm of the opinion that there are five stages of drunk-watching. First we laugh, or at least sometimes we do. After a while the drunk's shenanigans make us shake our heads and wonder. At some point, we begin to moan, even grimace ("Yikes, that's gotta hurt"). Then come the groans. ("Oh, please stop before you hurt yourself and/or someone else irreparably.") Finally, we hope the drunk will terminate their actions before it's too late. Too often it's too late and something—or someone—has been destroyed.

I wonder if the reader will agree with my breakdown.

Are you still laughing?

Can you hear a moan? A groan?

What should become of this last bunch? The destroyers?

Put down your drink, have a read.

The throne room is a good place to read. It's a room all too familiar to many drunks. Or gather your friends around to share the stories. Yeah, they are all true.

Then write to me at *bill@wispid.com* and tell me what you think.

LAUGHERS

NAKED SLEEPWALKERS ON THE RISE

Travelodge of London says its 300 business hotels are being over-run, um, walked, with naked sleepwalkers... 95% of them men.

The zombies show up at the front desk asking for a newspaper, for directions to the bathroom, to check out... but never for a towel to cover up.

Consequently, Travelodge is training their night staff on how to deal with the problem... starting with the towel.

Most fellows NEED covering up.

Sleepwalking is caused by...

1. booze

2. stress

3. eating cheese

4. too much caffeine

Nervous day after work, spiked coffee and some Brie... see you at the front desk.

FAKE LAWYER DEFENDS DRUNK DRIVER

A drunk took his stupidity with him when he went to hire counsel.

The drunk paid $18,000 in legal fees to hire what turned out to be a fake lawyer.

The jury deliberated just eight minutes before convicting the drunk.

When the fake lawyer screened for potential jurors, he asked, "If you were in a forest and you came to a clearing, and you saw a house, could you describe the house?"

Another juror was asked if s/he consumed alcohol like the frat brothers in 'Animal House.'

And yet another juror was asked if s/he liked animals.

The prosecutor decided after this barrage of unusual questions to check on the phony defense counsel.

Counsel is now in need of counsel… the fake faces charges of first-degree larceny and forgery.

DRUNKEN HALLOWEENIE MISTAKEN FOR DEAD

A 24-year-old fellow, on a train in Bad Segeberg, fell into a drunken stupor on his way home from a Halloween party.

His hands and head were smeared with blood (fake) but passengers thought he had been murdered and left there. They tried but failed to wake him up.

The police, however, succeeded in raising the man from the dead, made him wash off his make-up and sent him on his way.

Bad Segeberg… Bad Segeberg!

83-YEAR-OLD FOUND GUILTY OF SOLICITATION

An 83-year-old man, who can't believe his luck—bad luck—was found guilty by a jury of soliciting a prostitute.

The WWII vet says, "I'm a virgin all the way."

The undercover cop says he told her, "I have money," and offered him $20 to perform a sex act.

The old codger, who also claims to be hard of hearing, says he was involved in a 'commotion' and the woman (cop) was 'making eyes' at him. 'Next thing I know—what the hell is this?'

A courtroom… a judge… attorneys… stenographers… reporters… a guilty verdict… That's what it is.

The fiasco started with… a few beers on Thursday afternoon.

Go figure.

'LEGLESS' MAN FINDS HIS LEGS

It must have been the cops that had a bit too much.

The 'legless' man was a paraplegic who did indeed still have his legs.

He was steering. His friend was working the gas pedal and brakes when they were stopped.

Both were drunk—the driver had 0.16 and the pedal worker 0.09 blood alcohol, above the 0.08 limit.

The police clocked them at 35 mph in a 55-mph zone.

We are left to wonder, if the police got the part about the legs wrong, what else might not be correct in their report?

Still… drinking and driving…

Have fun in court, guys.

DRUNK AS A SKUNK ON A CONVEYOR BELT

A Russian, who apparently could NOT hold his vodka, fell asleep on a makeshift bed… a conveyor belt at the Beijing Capital International Airport.

Good news for him, he wasn't lost with other luggage in Timbuktu.

Police said he 'smelled like a distillery.'

He was taken to an emergency aid center where he was sobered up and released.

Meanwhile, the plane he was to board is long gone.

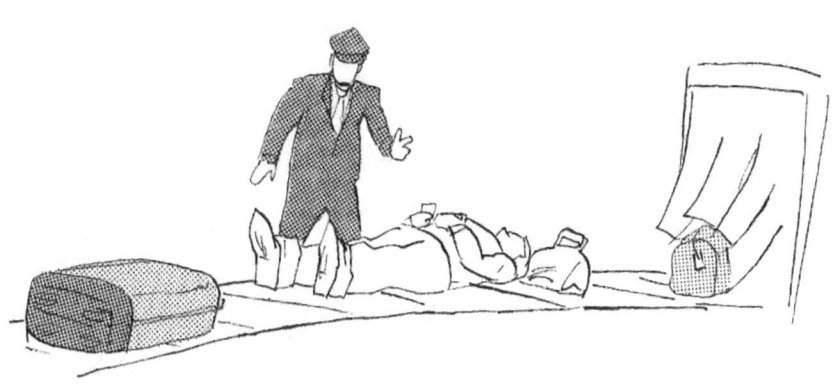

DRINKING BEER DRIVES ELEPHANTS BONKERS, TOO

In India, six of the elephants in a herd big enough to make up a football team got drunk on some rice beer.

After which, they decided to uproot a utility pole, not considering there were power lines connected to it.

Sounds like something most drunks would do... eh?

The part-wall, part-pillar, part-rope, part-snake big fellows got electrocuted... six of the 40.

The others were chased away by the villagers.

Let's see ...hungry... thirsty... drunk... yank... ZZZZttt!!... dead!

Change elephant to most any boozer and guess what the result might be..

LAW STUDENT SHOOTS LAW BOOK

An Indiana University law student took aim and fired at one of his law textbooks—on real estate transfer finance and developments.

The book had two bullet holes in it, and the 27-year-old student who shot it is facing a felony charge of criminal recklessness.

The student, not surprisingly… under the influence of alcohol.

In his apartment—two assault rifles, an AR-15 and an AK-47.

DRUNK DRIVER WITH FLAT TIRE CALLS POLICE

"Well, I thought I was calling the breakdown service," he slobbered.

Instead, a drunk in Austria called the police emergency number.

The man no longer needs help with his car. Rather, he needs help getting his license back.

DRINKING AND LAWN MOWING DON'T MIX

A drunk dude tried to outrun the police on his lawn mower.

The lawn-mowing knothead was caught by the police who chased him down... on foot.

The guy wouldn't take a sobriety test, but police concluded that the case of beer he had strapped to his vehicle might have some connection to his erratic driving unskills.

The knucklehead now faces a year in jail for obstructing a police officer and DUI.

How do you raise the fun level when you are mowing the lawn?

DRUNKEN MAN SCREWS AND IS FORCED TO MARRY A GOAT... AND PAY THE DOWRY

A man who was 'drunk at the time' was found doing the dirty with a goat.

The owner of the goat forced the man to pay 25 pounds and marry the goat as punishment.

The goat later had a kid... the man was NOT the father... we hope.

The goat died eventually, but the man, who wishes he had not been drinking at the time, must continue to live with the shame.

BEER CANS FLYING AT 115 MPH, THE FINGER AND A TASER

A 26-year-old redneck in FL was having a ball… for a while.

He zipped along at speeds of up to 115 mph in his truck in heavy rainfall.

He threw beer cans out the window in the process.

When cops pulled alongside, he showed them who was cool… by giving them the finger.

When the cops finally did get him pulled over, he reached to show them what else he had in his glove box.

The police showed him their Taser and how it works.

He's now in jail. Using methamphetamines and drinking booze all day and taunting the police will get you there.

Good thing is… he is still alive.

DRUNK AND STUPID IN SOUTH AFRICA

Two thieves swiped a hearse, with corpse inside, and went barhopping.

When the hearse ran out of gas, the two knuckleheads were able to persuade three women to help them push the car to a gas station.

"If you help push, I'll let you ride in the back with Joe. He's no trouble, doesn't drink any and I guarantee he'll keep his hands off you."

The women were told that "Joe" was a relative and they were on their way to bury him.

But, the women didn't buy it… if they were the kind of woman who could be picked up in a bar and persuaded to help push a hearse, they were NOT the kind of women who wanted to be left alone by Joe or anyone else.

Police caught up with the two who admitted they hadn't dumped the corpse yet because they had yet to decide what to do with the car.

"Gee, it's hard to figure things out when you are drunk."

DRUNK MAN CAUGHT STEALING FLOWERS FROM A HEARSE

"Gee, I wish I had been drinking at the time" is something we never hear.

A 37-year-old fellow... drunk as a skunk... on his way home maybe? in need of some way to appease the little lady? again? broke into a hearse that was being used for a funeral and started stealing flowers and vases that were inside.

Police were called to Our Lady of Guadalupe Church in Flagstaff to apprehend the man, who had been detained by the mortician.

"Stop, or I will fill your veins with other stuff besides your blood!"

"Uh... are you my mommy?"

Drunk + stupid = drunpid!

DRUNK MAN GETS STUCK IN EX-GIRLFRIEND'S CHIMNEY

This is the second guy in a week to get stuck in a chimney.

A drunk man had to be rescued when he got stuck trying to climb down a chimney of his former girlfriend at about 3:30 a.m..

Amazingly, the drunk stumbled upon something I have been saying all along…

"Everyone does stupid things sometimes when they're drunk."

But, I would go one step further… people are stupid for getting drunk and then comes more stupidity = drunpidity.

The girlfriend received a misdemeanor citation for blocking the fireplace.

She "told them to leave him in the chimney and let him die."

After the man was treated at the hospital, he went BACK.

He's stupid even when he is sober!

His ex hit him with a garbage can and pelted him with bottles while yelling, "Get off my porch, and don't you ever come back here."

He was later spotted with a shovel.

Man Loses His Pants With $41K+ in the Pockets

I have heard of losing your shirt but ….this guy says he doesn't know what happened between when he left the bar and when he woke up the next morning.

The police didn't want to believe the guy either, until he gave them the exact amount… a cashier's check for $41,093 and several hundred dollars in cash were in the pants.

A dog had found the pants at an intersection, and when the owner of the dog tried unsuccessfully to deliver the britches to their owner at home, he turned them over to the police who then contacted the man.

"I woke up cold not knowing where the heck I was, and I didn't realize it at first because I still had my shoes and socks on," he said. "When I got up, I realized, my God, I don't have any pants."

Yeah… now we know why mom, or was it dad, or probably both, always said, "Keep your pants on."

DRUNKEN MAN CAUGHT HAVING SEX WITH A FENCE

A drunken man was caught by policemen in London trying to have sex with a fence.

The man told police, "I'm going to have sex with that fence."

Police told him they were taking him in.

Last week it was a guy caught half-naked with his bicycle in a hotel.

WOMAN INSISTS HER CIGARETTES ARE AN ID

When the woman was asked to give her ID, she showed the police a pack of cigarettes.

"Thash me!"

When the cops showed up, an intoxicated woman and another drunken fellow were knocking each other about.

The woman had taken the men's car and they wanted it back.

In the end, when the woman wakes up from her hangover, she'll learn she is charged with grand theft and battery....

And, well, maybe she had a face like a camel, so the cops decided to not charge her with using a fake ID.

DRUNK GETS CAUGHT SCREWING STUFFED DOG

A man with a history of getting himself in trouble when he has been drinking, got himself in trouble again.

He moved from garage to garage, swiping things, until he came upon a stuffed toy dog.

"He was lying there with his genitalia exposed next to the stuffed dog," said an attorney. "While the police report doesn't describe it this way, the dog might be appropriately characterized as now being anatomically correct, as opposed to its condition before he removed it."

The man has been sentenced to six months in jail… sans dog.

BURGLAR IS DRUNKEN NEIGHBOR

A man, I'll call him Bob, was arrested for trespassing.

Bob, who was too drunk to recognize that his key did not work the door, that his house was a different color, and that his dog was gone, broke into a home and sat down on the furniture he did not know was not his. When the real owner (I'll call him Mike) came home, Bob offered him a drink.

Bob's house was two doors down.

Instead of spending the night sleeping in his bed, Bob slept in one paid for by the city.

SHAKERS

World Leader of Pernod Ricard Group Warns Against Drunk Driving

I'd never heard of the Pernod Ricard Group based in Paris. But then, I don't know much about booze at all, except the many stupid things people do when they have too much, and that I lost a brother and sister who both had too much… on different days in different places.

The CEO of Pernod Ricard was in Korea to promote a "Smart Driving: Don't Drink & Drive" campaign going into the year-end holiday season in that country.

The CEO says, "his company has every reason to pay attention to that social issue (responsible drinking)."

Indeed they do have a responsibility.

Unfortunately, the people who need to heed his warning are most likely too soused to pay attention.

Please don't drink and drive, don't drink and shoot, don't drink and drop your kids from balconies…

If you drink… please, just don't do anything else… nothing else… NOTHING!

HIGH SCHOOL GIRLS PASS VODKA AROUND CLASSROOM IN A WATER BOTTLE

It's obvious these girls haven't read this little pamphlet.

Frankly, I think this book should be required reading for high school kids… especially these four girls who were passing vodka around their classroom in a water bottle… during science class.

An experiment of some sort?

Three of the girls who passed the bottle around were 14 and one was 15 years old.

The teacher eventually noticed the kids wouldn't follow her instructions, that is, wear goggles when instructed. So, the teacher called the vice principal in.

The vice principal took one girl away but noticed she kept stumbling down the stairs.

She was later found to have a blood alcohol level of .172.

Good thing she wasn't driving.

The school says it will NOT prohibit water bottles because of the four girls' actions.

"We might change the policy for these four offenders but we don't want to punish 1,400 students."

A school policy that makes sense?!

DRUNKFEST FAILS TO SOLVE LOVE TRIANGLE

Two 20-something-year-old women in love with the same man decided, instead of cutting the man in half as Solomon might recommend, to have a drinking contest.

Each woman was challenged to drink three bottles of strong wine in three hours.

They did, both of them.

Both women simultaneously collapsed and had to be taken by ambulance to emergency care.

The result—a draw.

And, another round.

The guy, meanwhile… on a date maybe?

PRINCETON UNIVERSITY STUDENTS ARRESTED FOR DRUNK GOLF-CART DRIVING

Driving a golf cart around campus at 2:20 a.m., fast enough to roll the thing and throw your buddy out, are good indications that the driver's ability may be impaired somewhat (a lot?).

Hitting a police car is a dead giveaway.

Thankfully, the two 21-year-olds didn't have to die.

However, one was arrested on the spot… too drunk to run, perhaps?

The other was picked up a few days later.

See you in court, fellows.

4-YEAR-OLD CHILD GETS REPOSSESSED

When kids go bonkers, parents will sometimes accuse them of being possessed.

So, when a child gets hauled away, does that mean the possessed are repossessed?

The story doesn't make sense to me, since the car that was being repossessed was at the home of an acquaintance of the driver doing the hauling... but, what also doesn't make sense is how'd nobody see the 4-year-old kid in the back seat before they hauled it away?

And, where was the kid's mom or dad?

Driver: "Duh, uh... we checked the back seat and we didn't see nothin'."

Mom: "I thought little Fashawn was playing in the back yard, not hiding in the SUV."

A driver following the two trucks noticed—

"Hey, somebody just fell out of the back of the car!"

And, they let these people drive cars?!

And, they let these parents have kids?!

PiLoT DiSQUALiFiED FoR DRiNKiNG BEFoRE FLiGHT

An All Nippon Airways pilot was grounded from flight duties for drinking alcohol 9.5 hours BEFORE a flight.

He violated in-house rules that prohibit crew members from drinking within 12 hours of a flight.

Going down with the 38-year-old Airbus A320 captain were three of his superiors, including the deputy in charge of flight operations and another pilot who didn't speak up.

The captain had a few drinks at 10 p.m. the night before he flew four flights that started at 7:25 a.m. the next morning.

The incident came to light just last month… the actual infraction was last year in September… when an acquaintance of the captain reported the incident.

He is now… pushing papers.

DRIVING DRUNK WITH A 2-YEAR-OLD IN THE BACK SEAT

A 40-year-old dad was:

1. driving drunk

2. holding an open 24-oz. container of Bud Light

3. not wearing a seat belt

4. in an uninsured car

5. driving with an expired inspection

6. using the wrong license plates on the car

7. heading west in an eastbound lane

8. letting his little 2-year-old flop about in the back seat unrestrained

9. taken to jail and is being held without bail.

DRUNKEN BURGLAR LEAVES NAME IN GRAFFITI

Yup... bad guys like to leave a mark, something to let everyone know it was them IF they ever get caught. But, they don't expect to get caught... unless... the mark they leave happens to be their name.

"Peter Addison was here" was written by an 18-year-old drunken burglar.

Of "The Adlington Massiv" gang.

Coppers in Britain are saying, "There are some pretty stupid criminals around, but to leave your own name at the scene of the crime takes the biscuit. The daftness of this lad certainly made our job a lot easier."

Yeah... don't you like it when a day goes so smoothly at work sometimes?

The boy pleaded guilty and is serving out his punishment.

7 Bottles of Booze Downed in 15 Minutes at Wal-Mart

After 16 months of being on the wagon, a man in Waukesha (I don't know where that's at) fell off quickly and hard… in 15 minutes, he guzzled seven bottles of 12-oz. Jack Daniels Lynchburg Lemonade.

Security videos caught him, said Mukwonago (I don't know where this is either) police.

The man was not scared that the police caught him, not saddened that he went on a drunken binge… he stated, "I don't know how I am going to tell my wife."

Finance Bureaucrats Arrested for Gang-rape

Two Finance Ministry Bureaucrats needed to get out of their stuffy funk... the wrong way.

The 34- and 28-year-olds gang-raped a Tokyo woman in her apartment.

One denies the allegations and the other has admitted to them.

The two men picked up the woman at about 1 a.m. and went to—surprise—drink at a nearby pub.

The two drunks asked the woman to let her stay with them until the morning train... and the rest is stupid... she, them, drinking... rape... lies... arrest... jail...

JR. HIGH SCHOOL TEACHER TAKES NUDE PHOTOS OF STUDENT

A 27-year-old junior high school teacher was fired for taking nude pictures of one of his students… then molesting her… or the other way around.

Teach was then placed under arrest for violating ordinances protecting youths and the Law Punishing Acts Related to Child Prostitution and Child Pornography.

The teacher and student apparently had interacted on a 'number of occasions.'

Um… where were the parents of this new teenager while the teacher was doing the misdeeds? Huh?!

Another teacher… 56 years old… forced to resign for a DUI….

Great example these Japanese teachers set, eh?

STUDENT GOVERNMENT SPOKESMAN CHARGED WITH DUI

A Bloomsburg University student president had enough.

He wrote a letter to the Press Enterprise of Bloomsburg about media coverage of the college's annual Block Party.

The student prez wrote, stories have "painted BU students with a broad and negative brush and are both inaccurate and extremely unfair to the thousands of responsible, mature Bloomsburg students who are an asset to the school and this community."

Then he went out and celebrated by getting drunk.

The cops pulled him over for going 50 mph in a 15-mph zone, and a breath test showed he had .147 blood-alcohol level… over the .08 legal limit.

He was charged with a DUI, speeding and careless driving.

I guess what he meant to say was that the president of the student government could play by different rules than the student body….

But that sort of thing doesn't happen in the real world, does it?

Yeah, right.

TOO DRUNK TO GET MEDICAL ATTENTION AFTER BEING ATTACKED BY A CROCODILE

They are tough down under.

A 35-year-old dude in Australia drank 12 cans of beer... a 'half a slab.'

Then... he decided to go into the drink. He dove in and landed on top of an crocodile.

The croc got the best of him but left him alive and in need of about 40 stitches.

The man, too drunk to go to the hospital, decided to sleep it off for about seven hours and then go.

By the time he got there, he was bleeding so profusely he had to use his blanket to sop up the blood... and the alcohol in his blood.

DRUNK BEATS TAXI DRIVER AND STEALS HIS CAB

A 28-year-old bank employee assaulted a taxi driver and stole his cab in the early hours… just before 2 a.m.

All was well… the guy had called the taxi to get a ride home… smart so far.

But, then the drunk fell asleep.

When the taxi driver woke him up to ask him where his home was, the man got irate, hit the driver in the face and stomach, and then escaped with the car.

The police later found the car and the drunk wobbling around nearby.

That is NOT why drunks are told to take a taxi home if they are too soused to drive. Now, is it?

Beer Party for Teenagers

51-year-old Mrs. Robinson threw a big beer party for teenagers after the local high school homecoming dance.

And Simon & Garfunkel's hit… "Here's to you Mrs. Robinson"… played in the background?

Mrs. R, said "It was a big mistake!"

Really, now.

"I just wanted to provide a safe environment for the kids to hang out and drink."

And what part of drinking makes the environment safe?

I "took all of their car keys and made it clear that everyone who was drinking would have to stay the night at her house."

Deputies found cases and cases of beer, empty and stacked in the laundry room.

Mrs. R said she "lost total control of the situation."

Gosh, and do we wonder how that might have happened?

Charged with "contributing to the delinquency of a minor and allowing minors alcohol at an open house party."

OFF-DUTY COP SNATCHES WOMAN'S PURSE

Alcohol is the social lubricant in Japan, it is said.

It also works to loosen up cops, too.

The Japanese will do the strangest things after sipping a beer. If their actions become offensive, they blame the booze. If not, then they just roll with it.

A cop had a beer with some friends at the police station before heading home.

On his way home, he snatched a bag from a woman in the upscale Roppongi district in Tokyo.

An arrest followed… his… and he couldn't blame it on the social lubricant, either.

DRUNKEN U.S. SAILOR WRESTLES PASSERBY

I was stationed in Yokosuka when I was in the U.S. Navy.

There were a LOT of knuckleheads like this guy who decided to assault a passerby by putting him into a headlock.

The 23-year-old sailor assaulted a 43-year-old from behind.

The seaman wobbled, refused a Breathalyzer test, and announced that he didn't remember what he did to the 43-year-old fellow.

However, he did think, "Gee, I sure am glad I was drinking at the time."

How many international incidents have been caused, I wonder, because one or both sides of the parties involved thought it would be a good idea to share a drink together?

TAXI WHISPERER SCARES PASSENGERS

The taxi whisperer... a distant relative of the horse whisperer... was giving passengers the creeps.

In China, a woman passenger started getting freaked out when she heard voices in the back of the car.

The driver stopped to look around when he finally found a drunk in the trunk mumbling to himself and... who did NOT know how he had gotten there.

Police let him go after he sobered up.

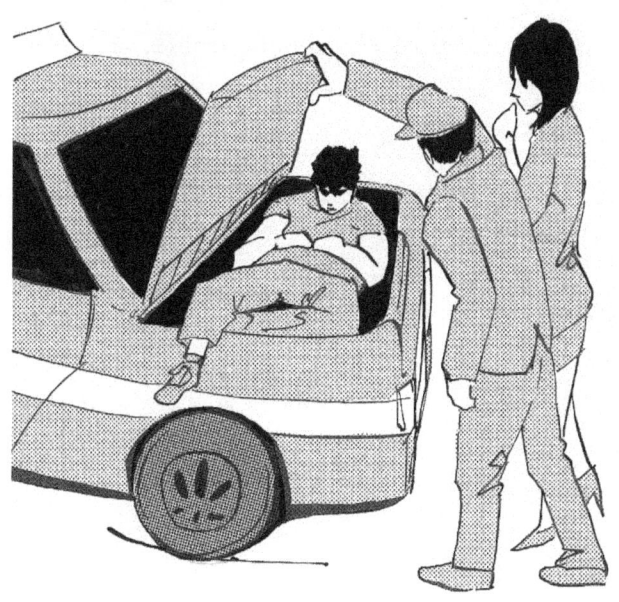

POLICE CHIEF CHARGED WITH SEXUAL ASSAULTS

"If you don't stop that, I will call the police!"

"I am the police. And, so are you."

"Well, then. I'll call the police chief!!"

"I am the police chief, you idiot."

In the end, the real idiot is a ten-year veteran police chief who was charged with two counts of sexual assault against male employees.

The police chief was suspended WITH PAY!

Where is Reader's Digest and the THAT'S OUTRAGEOUS writers when you need them?

He's in jail because no one has come up with the $200,000 bond.

Do the other inmates know who he is and why he is there?

Get this… the chief is accused of performing oral sex on another male employee who had passed out drunk at a party.

"Gee, I wish I had been drinking at the time…."

The police chief used an instrument to violate another employee AFTER he (the employee) had passed out, also drunk… but at a different party.

And, somebody please remind me again, why is it that people drink?

The city manager weighed in, "This will reflect poorly on us."

What… employees getting drunk and violated, or police chiefs doing the violating, or both?

COUPLE LEAVES KIDS IN SUV TO DRINK MARGARITAS

A couple, 33 and 26 years old, left their 1-year-old boy and 5-month-old girl in their Ford Expedition at around 8 p.m. while they went into the restaurant to sip margaritas for about half an hour.

Mom said she drove there drunk with the children in the car.

When asked if she regretted her actions—nope was the reply.

Passersby alerted the police.

The children were turned over to a family member and the poor excuse for parents—one is free on $10,000 bond and the other is being held in jail on $7,500 bond.

Moaners

4 FOOTBALL PLAYERS SHELVED FOR DRINKING SPREE

Four professional football players in Korea were suspended from national matches for a year.

They were also ordered to complete 80 hours of community service.

Their offense… a midnight drinking spree during a regional tournament.

The four ball players went into a karaoke bar in Jakarta to drink off an upset loss to Bahrain and be entertained by female hostesses.

Now they get to watch from the sidelines and work to keep themselves in shape.

Were the drinks worth it, boys?

ONE VERY GOOD REASON WHY COUPLES WHO DIVORCE SHOULD NOT LIVE TOGETHER

I've been divorced. It wasn't fun.

However, I didn't need to go to school or get professional help to know that, after divorce, it is NOT a good idea for the couple to continue to live together.

Here's very strong evidence why:

A Russian woman set fire to her ex-husband's penis as he sat naked watching TV and drinking vodka.

(Yet another guy who will never say, "Gee! I wish I had been drinking at the time.")

The couple divorced three years ago, but continued to share their flat—perhaps a necessity in Russia, where property costs are so high. (And why does it cost so much for land in a country two times bigger than the number-two-sized country in the world? I dunno.)

The man said, "It was monstrously painful. I don't know what I did to deserve this."

Let's see… divorced, naked, in front of the TV, drinking… gee, I wonder what he did to deserve it.

Still… that's gotta hurt.

How often do you sit around naked with your ex running around?

PET GOATS SHOT FOR LACK OF BEER

The man told his daughter to tell her mother to bring some beer home.

When mom refused, dad got angry and got his gun, the one he had just been using from a day of hunting.

Sure enough, mom came home without the beer, and dad went after one of the two pet goats.

Mom and daughter heard four gun shots.

When they went outside, the goat's guts were hanging out but the animal was still alive.

Four gun shots and he couldn't kill a non-moving goat!?

No wonder the guy wanted a beer after a day of hunting.

He was found and arrested in a bar later in the day.

STRIP CLUB PATRON SETS EMPLOYEE ON FIRE

I can't remember the last time I read about something good coming out of a strip club, or somebody saying, "Gee, I'm glad I was at the strip club last night…"

Some guy, who had been kicked out of a strip club for trying to take pictures of the girls, returned with gasoline and a match.

He poured it on another employee of the strip club, not one of the girls, and burned the guy—2nd- and 3rd-degree burns over more than 80% of his body..

Drunk, too?

DRUNK WOMAN LETS HER 5-YEAR-OLD SON DRIVE

A 24-year-old woman was arrested for letting her 5-year-old son drive while she sat back in a drunken stupor.

The boy's 3-year-old brother was crawling around on the back seat of the car.

Police weren't reassured when they asked the woman if she was okay and is this your toddler and she responded, "Yes, but he's a good driver."

The woman admitted to taking Percocet, a painkiller that she needed when the kids acted up, and vodka.

The boy confessed to not being such a good driver: "My legs were too short to reach the pedals."

Still… when he grows up, "I want to be a race car driver."

Yeah… maybe, if his mom doesn't kill him first.

Another reason why we never hear, "Gee, I wish I had been drinking at the time."

OKTOBERFEST PARTIER GETS STUCK IN CHIMNEY FOR 12 HOURS

A German dude had a great time getting soused at Munich's Oktoberfest. That is, until he got stuck in a chimney for 12 hours.

When the 27-year-old came home, he couldn't find his friend. So, he climbed up on the roof (isn't that what you usually do when you can't get into a house?).

He thought he found a gap in the wall between the two houses, then fell about 100 feet headfirst into a chimney.

A janitor heard him calling for help about 12 hours later.

Somehow, he managed to get all of his clothes OFF to help him squeeze back up.

Firefighters are great men… pulling a drunk and naked guy out of a chimney who hadn't, presumably, been able to relieve himself for 12 hours.

PRINCIPAL UNDRESSES DRUNK WOMAN IN BAR

I can't figure out which category this belongs in... drunk and stupid, or sex and stupid.

A 49-year-old deputy principal of a junior high school invited a 26-year-old woman to a bar in Tokyo.

After the young lady got drunk and passed out... the old geezer took off her clothes, underwear, too and took pictures of her with his cell phone camera.

They didn't know each other but had met at a train stop after the old fellow, drunk, had fallen asleep and missed his stop.

To pass the time before the next train came... the two went to a bar.

It seems... the old guy occupied himself more in the passing of time.

Drunk and stupid, or sex and stupid?

COP CRASHES CAR ON NATIONAL HIGHWAY

A police investigator crashed his car on a national highway while driving... drunk.

He had drunk four or five glasses of shochu (a sake-like drink) before driving.

Let's see, if kids are driving drunk, we know who we do NOT want to send now, don't we?

ASSOCIATE PROFESSOR LOSES JOB OVER SEXUAL HARASSMENT OF TWO FEMALE STUDENTS

A 40-year-old Shimane University associate professor resigned after he sexually harassed two female students.

First, he served a three-month suspension... then he called it quits.

Shimane University has had three instructors punished in the past two years for sexual harassment.

His crime: "you have a good figure." And—he touched their hair.

However, on another occasion—drunk, of course—he kicked one woman and yanked the other's muffler during a drinking party.

When the students had had enough... they brought the issue to university authorities who, after a fact-finding session, decided the prof was guilty.

I wonder... does he really think it was worth it... getting drunk with his students?

RAPE, ABUSE, ARSON—
BUT NOT THE PICTURES!

The 19-year-old endured rape by her brother… abuse… from her brother… but when he burned down their mother's house… no mas!

A judge convicted her now 28-year-old brother of incest and assault.

The woman said she came home to find her brother drinking. (WARNING!).

He asked her to join him. (WARNING!)

When she wanted to stop, he pressured her to drink more. (WARNING! WARNING!!)

When she woke up, she found her brother having sex with her. (YUCK!)

The woman didn't report the rape or a subsequent incident when he choked and kicked her because she was a "forgive and forget" person.

However, last year, her brother came home drunk (WARNING!) and burned their mother's house down.

She lost ultrasound pictures of her baby and their (late) dad.

That was the last straw.

BANKER RAPES, MOLESTS INTERVIEWEES... GOES DIRECTLY TO JAIL

A former bank employee (yeah, he was fired, thank goodness) has been sentenced to 4.5 years in jail.

He raped one female university student applicant for a job at the bank where he worked, and molested two others.

The former employee of the Bank of Tokyo-Mitsubishi talked his victims into joining him for dinner to continue the interview process... then molested them.

The deeds were done AFTER the applicants and the interviewer went to a karaoke joint and AFTER he got them drunk...

GRADUATION PARTY COST
$53,000

Pop told his Georgia Tech graduating son he could blow $600 on a party with his friends.

Two months later they got the bill—for $53,000!—on their joint American Express credit card.

Dad says, "Their employees totally took advantage of my son."

Club's owner calls it "buyer's remorse after a huge champagne night of showing off in front of entertainers."

19 bottles of champagne from $150-$2000 each and Monopoly-like money used to tip waitresses giving lap dances added up… way up.

24 of the 30 receipts were printed after 4 a.m. when the club should have been sending people out the door.

The young man… had been drinking heavily BEFORE he got to the club.

Go! Dad!

PRIEST GETS DRUNK, DRIVES AND PUNCHES COP

Mexico City is apparently cracking down on drunken drivers… priests included.

A priest, identified by his papers and clutching a prayer book, was pulled over for driving erratically.

When the cops said they were going to tow his car… he went after them with fisticuffs.

A few hours in jail and his fine paid in full, the priest is off to mass and wine and…

"Yo, Padre. We're gonna have to tow your car."

"Noth on my rife. Take dissss!"

Bare-Breasted Barmaid Crushes Beer Cans. Yeah, With Those!

They are tougher than I thought down under.

A barmaid carries a beer can crusher under her blouse.

She whipped the two puppies out to show patrons that she could indeed crush beer cans with her breasts while hanging spoons from her nipples.

Try that!

The little lady pleaded guilty and was fined $900… the hotel manager, too.

My bet is that they made MUCH MORE off of bets she couldn't do it in the first place.

The local police: "It sends a clear message to all licensees in Peel that we will not tolerate this type of behavior in our licensed premises."

I dunno, seems to me, it could mean great business for the district, no?

COP CHASES CAR... COPS CATCH CAR... DRUNK SLEEPS IN CAR

The car just kind of idled along... while the driver slept.

The cop chased it, on foot... while the driver slept.

A cop jumped onto the running board and reached in and steered the car... while the driver slept.

The cop finally got the car to stop by putting it into neutral and coasting... while the driver slept.

The cops woke the man up... drunk and no license.

DRUNKEN TRAIN CONDUCTOR FLASHES PRIVATE PARTS

The West Japan Railway Co. employee was NOT showing the passengers where the brakes were, the speedometer or the intercom system... or even the private room where they get to rest.

He flashed his private parts... the 50-year-old undid his pants and let junior out.

When he was arrested he confessed—drunk at the time, he didn't remember what he did on the train.

Another dude to join the ranks of those who will never say, "Gee, I wish I had been drinking at the time."

GRANDMA GIVES GIN TO 9-YEAR-OLD GRANDCHILD

I guess we'd all better think twice about asking Granny to watch the kids.

A 47-year-old grandmother is suspected of giving her grandchild two drinks from a gin bottle in hopes that the little girl would pass out so she, grandma, could go out.

Mom was working a 12-hour shift at the time.

An anonymous tip got the police to the apartment, and a breath test showed the girl had an alcohol level of 0.42%, half the legal limit for driving. No consolation there… the 9-year-old was already home.

The test, however, was taken 8 hours after the drinks were given to her.

The little girl remembered vomiting, hitting her head, then blacking out.

Yeah… that's pretty much how it goes when you have too much to drink.

The grandmother is in jail… and should be left there.

Well… at least grandma did get to go out.

HARD-CORE ALCOHOLIC BUSTED FOR DRINKING HAIR SPRAY AT WAL-MART

A man was busted for drinking two cans of hair spray for the alcohol in it at a Wal-Mart.

The hair spray cost $1.92, and the man had $15 in his pocket.

The hard-core alcoholic said, "The temptation was too great" to NOT drink the hair spray, which he had done on several occasions before.

The man was under surveillance. He had previously done the same thing.

He came in to fill a prescription. While waiting, he would take a bottle of hair spray to the garden center and chug it down. Then, rinse and repeat.

Anybody thirsty?

Let's head to Wal-Mart.

NORTHWESTERN UNIVERSITY ENGINEERING GRADS INVENT BINGE-DRINKING DEVICE

It's good to know that our graduate students at one of America's finest, Northwestern University, are putting their biomedical engineering learning to, um, 'good use.'

Two students have created a Beer Pong Rubber that they are selling for $9.99.

The triangular shaped rubbers prevent plastic beer cups from slipping or moving when the drinking game is played—throwing or bouncing a ping-pong ball into an opponent's glass means the owner of the cup must guzzle down the beer.

Now, students can play the game and not make as big a mess as before… until they lose and throw up all over the place.

How about somebody inventing a bib that college students can wear to catch the discharge when they puke their guts out?

Oh boy, students in training who will grow up to never say, "Gee, I wish I had been drinking at the time."

KYOTO UNIVERSITY PROF. DRUNK, FORGETS TO PAY, ARRESTED!

A professor of one of Japan's most prestigious universities, Kyoto University, and head of the state-run university's Institute of Advanced Energy, got drunk—whiskey and beer.

No problem… nope, problem.

He left without paying the 12,000 bar tab ($100ish).

Police had to arrest the dude and make him pay up.

Yeah… he'll have a good story to share with his classroom on Monday, right?

GROANERS

COLLEGE FRATS ADD STRIPPER POLE TO HOUSE DECOR

School has started… get out the stripper poles.

Parents might be happy that the kids are away, getting an education, making good use of the $25K/year it's costing them to send little Jennie, Barbie or Katie to university.

"Might" is the key word…

If Pop knew that his little girl spent last weekend getting acquainted with the boys at the neighboring frat houses, he'd be plenty antsy. No doubt, that is where she was.

If Pop knew there was booze, plenty of it, flowing freely to loosen everyone up, he'd pace the floor. No doubt, his little girl was feeling pretty loose as well.

If Pop knew that the frat houses had installed stripper poles so that the guys could enjoy the evening more by watching the girls… Pop would be out the door.

Girls who use the pole say it gives them a sense of empowerment… that they've taken charge of their sexuality….

Uh… no!! It means they are drunk and entertaining a bunch of drunken college kids, is what it means.

Hurry, Pop!

COLLEGE FOOTBALL DRINKING VS. NEW YEAR'S EVE

UT-Austin has learned that college students drink more booze at football games than on New Year's Eve.

The same study also learned that women who had been drinking, even lightly, were more prone to engage in 'risky behavior.'

The weekly football schedule presented students with more regular opportunities.

Losses in high-profile games against conference or national rivals were more easily accepted when soused.

The study was funded by the National Institute of Alcohol Abuse and Alcoholism.

Let's see, and how much money was wasted on this study?

DRUNK CRACKS HEAD ON WALL

A drunk tried to take a short cut through a wall.

Yeah, he didn't make it.

Instead he cracked his head, slumped over and fell unconscious to the ground with his head bleeding.

Trying to run from the police… thud! Into the wall again.

In China, too, you never hear, "gee, I wish I had been drinking at the time."

60 PINTS OF BEER = MONTH-LONG HANGOVER

A Scottish dude, apparently quite capable of holding his own at the local pub, chugged down 60 pints.

For four weeks he complained of 'wavy' vision and a non-stop headache.

Doctors were stumped until an ophthalmologist observed:

1. swollen optical discs

2. greatly enlarged blind spots

3. "flame hemorrhages," or bleeding nerve fibres.

It took the man four days to consume the 60 pints (35 liters).

The man also suffered from severe dehydration.

Another clue might have been him spending six hours a day relieving himself, no?

Doctors treated him for six months—long-term blood-thinning—to restore his vision to normal and to get rid of the headaches.

Feeling better, he headed for the pub.

114,000 BOTTLES OF BEER ON THE WALL. DRUNKEN PARTY TONIGHT, AND TOMORROW AND THE NEXT DAY AND THE NEXT AND...

There's going to be a drunken party tonight... tomorrow... the day after... the next day and the next and the next....

I expect there will be lots of fodder and drunpidity as well.

In Mississauga, Ontario, 100,000 Moosehead Beers were stolen.

Somebody try and put that under your arm.

Two tractor-trailers with 70,000 cans and 44,000 bottles of Moosehead Lager were stolen.

The retail value of the beer—$197,000 (US).

Worse yet... Moosehead lovers will have to wait till next week to get the booze replenished.

It's the second time in three years Moosehead has been targeted, having lost 50,000 cans in 8/04 and only recovering 14,000 of the cans.

"We can't believe that of all the beer available in Canada that Moosehead would be targeted again," said a MH spokesman.

The common denominator... Moosehead and their security, or lack thereof.

3-Day Bender Finds Woman Passed Out in a Car

The cops woke the woman up.

She said… she didn't know how long she had been there or how she got there. She did remember that she was on a 3-day bender, though.

Her blood alcohol content was 5 times the legal limit.

Now… she has been placed in a mental health facility.

Anybody missing a mom? A grandma? A wife?

DRUNK TAUNTS POLICE

People do 'fun' things when they get drunk… like taunting the police.

A man called the police about 10 times from his cell phone:

"I'm hammered… come get me."

"I'm drunk and giving you guys clues and you still haven't found me."

"nah nah nah ne naaaah nah"

Two hours later, the drunpidiot pulled up in front of a couple of squad cars and taunted them some more.

Police caught up with him when his car broke down.

What's the most 'fun' you ever had drunk?

DRUNK AND NAKED ON I-95, SANS CAR

A PA dude was arrested by Delaware police because he was running naked and drunk on I-95.

He caused three accidents... none of them involving hitting him.

Two people tried to help the drunk streaker, but he attacked them in return.

Now he faces two counts of assault and one of being drunk on the highway... sans car.

He's locked up now.

GIRL-ON-GIRL ASTROLUBE WRESTLING

When people talk about what is NOT illegal, it usually means they are pushing the limits.

A young woman, not yet 21, contacted police saying she was pressured into taking part in a wrestling match with her friend at… you guessed it… a bar … in Colorado.

The young lady—yup—had been served alcohol.

I don't know whether she lost and that was her beef, or that she found herself in tight clothes, slip-sliding around in a pit while drunken bozos cheered/leered on.

One thing is for sure… the booze was the 'lubricant' that got her into the predicament in the first place.

I learned a long time ago to stay away from the gray areas. If it's legal… good. If it's illegal… bad. If people are haggling and the police are scratching their heads over whether it is not illegal or whatnot… then stay away.

Kind of like sin… if you think it is wrong… it is probably is. If you think it might be wrong… turn around. There is enough right to do in the world that we need not play, even in a pit with Astrolube all over, to keep ourselves occupied.

SEX WITH THE SIDEWALK

An 18-year-old horny kid simulated having sex on/with the sidewalk.

Of course, the knucklehead had drunk a half bottle of vodka before giving it a try.

Before that, passing motorists saw him lying on his back relieving sexual tension, after which he rolled over and continued on.

A neighbor intervened and took the boy home, who now finds his name on the sex offenders register.

And if he succeeded with the sidewalk and they reproduced, what would he tell the baby sidewalk? "Be sure to stay out from under weird kids passing by with body parts hanging out."

DAD DRIVES DRUNK, MOM SHOWS UP TO GET THE KIDS... DRUNK

Dad had his 12-year-old son in the car when police pulled him over for running a red light.

His breath measured 0.11 on the breath test, above the 0.8 legal standard.

The police asked the boy to call his mom to come get them.

She did... she came with their 9-year-old daughter... but... mom was drunk, too. 0.13.

The parents were held until they sobered up, and the kids were turned over to a relative... a sober one, we presume.

Way to go, Dad!

Good job, Mom!

Kids don't have a chance, do they?

'COOL' MOM HELPS KIDS PASS BEER FROM MOVING SUV

"My mom is way cooler than your mom."

"Yeah, well, your mom can be cool in jail."

Mom… was driving the cheerleaders to a high school game when another car full of boys who were fools came driving nearby.

'Beer?'

Mom, driving a school van, drove by close enough to the other car that the boys could pass them a beer… see, she is cool.

It was two weeks after the fact that somebody tipped off the school as to just how cool the mom was/is.

The girls have been suspended. Mom no longer drives for the school.

Instead, they sit home together and be… cool.

ROBBING CANDY FROM A BABY

Two women in Anchorage worked in cahoots to rob seven trick-or-treaters of their candy on Halloween.

One woman, 20, is charged and the other is still at large.

Two masked thieves got out of their truck, fired a gun and took the candy from the kids... and their iPhone, too.

The children... got the truck's license plate number.

Things started out for the robbers at Latitude 62... a bar and restaurant.

Well, if they aren't drinking in Alaska, what else is there to do? Get in trouble, it seems.

UF SORORITY DEGRADES UPSCALE COLUMBIA RESTAURANT

By the time the Columbia Restaurant staff kicked the girls and their dates out... all 250 or so of them... they had vomited everywhere, fought, broken the toilets, stolen from the bar and just plain got soused.

250 kids in semi-formal attire sounds like good money for a 102-year-old historic restaurant.

But... when 200 of them, many underage, showed up drunk, things went downhill real fast.

"The group turned our 102-year-old fine-dining restaurant into a frat house."

Yeah... drinking changes the way a lot of things look.

DRUNK OFFICIAL KICKS COP FOR CAB FARE

A Transport Official is being transported to the local pokey.

He was arrested for kicking a policeman when they squabbled over the fare for a taxi cab.

The drunk didn't want to pay, refused to understand... well, he was drunk...

The taxi cab driver couldn't get the money he was owed. The cab, which happened to be parked in front of a police box, got the attention of the policeman.

When the cop came over to try and settle things... the drunk kicked him.

Well... the drunk got kicked back... into jail for the night.

DRUNKEN SPORTS REPORTER BUSTED FOR MOLESTING WOMAN

A 40-year-old sports reporter fondled the butt of a 22-year-old woman while her 28-year-old boyfriend was standing by… at around 5:10 a.m.

His reason: "I wanted to have fun and show off," he told investigators.

The boyfriend overpowered the reporter, who committed the crime after drinking at a bar nearby.

"SPIKED DRINK MADE ME STRIP DOWN"

A man in Pennsylvania said he lost control of his senses due to a spiked drink... leading him to strip naked at a convenience store. (Drinking and thinking with the wrong head usually leads someone to lose control of their senses.)

The 26-year-old said he didn't realize what he was doing.

When? When he had the 'spiked drink,' or when he stripped naked.

Surveillance cameras caught the man coming in to prepay for gasoline... then stripping down and telling the female clerk, "I want everything."

DRUNK MAN DOWNS TWO VIALS OF BLOOD

A drunk man in Hong Kong told a court he was extremely thirsty.

In the cameras, you can see him "walk up to the laboratory counter, take three tubes containing blood samples, drink the contents of two and then dump the vials in the lift lobby."

When he realized what he drank, he rushed to a nearby commode and vomited it out.

The man got off for drinking the blood… but was jailed for theft.

"Give me a Bloody Mary, and hold the Mary," he slobbered out.

ELEMENTARY SCHOOL TEACHER GIVEN DUI ON HER WAY TO MORNING CLASSES

Hopefully, it wasn't for show-and-tell.

An elementary teacher was arrested for a DUI as she was driving to her morning classes.

Police stopped her in the parking lot of the elementary school where she teaches, after witnesses said they saw her swerving in the road and bouncing off of curbs… and not in a dodge car on the boardwalk.

The teacher of emotionally-challenged students had bloodshot eyes, slurred speech, a cold beer can and medication.

She told police officers she was suffering from a terminal disease… drunpidity it's called, I think.

Add drink to stupidity and your life is likely to be terminated at some point… sooner than you anticipate.

VOYEUR CAUGHT LOOKING DOWN ON TANNING WOMAN

I don't know if this guy is guilty of sexpidity or drunpidity….

A 43-year-old dude who said he was drunk at the time (his defense?) climbed up on a roof to look into a room "to see what people do in here," he said.

It's kind of like the guy who stood outside a couple's window because he wanted to see how normal people sleep.

The 22-year-old woman had stripped down, laid face up and, two minutes into her tanning session, saw somebody looking at her from above.

Scampering and grabbing of clothes followed… the guy wanted to see how she did that, too… he kept watching.

His lawyer got the man a suspended jail term by saying he was suffering from depression and had mental health problems …called sexpid and drunpid.

DESTROYERS

спиться (spit'sya) - to destroy one's life through drinking

Man Urinates on Dead, Disabled Woman

The 50-year-old disabled woman was already dead… from pancreatic failure.

A 27-year-old man shouted, "this is YouTube material," as he urinated on her.

Yeah… let's get a video of the man being locked in a jail cell while everyone else pisses all over him… and put it on YouTube.

The urinator… had been smoking pot and (sigh) drinking when he and two friends spotted her.

Before relieving himself on her, he poured a bucket of water on her and covered her with shaving cream.

The guy is off to court as everyone scratches their head and wonders what to charge him with.

Body Found in Heating Exhaust Duct at Elementary School

A 21-year-old man's body was found in the heating exhaust duct pipes at an elementary school in Anchorage, AK.

The man was last seen when he left his apartment about two weeks ago.

He had been drinking.

When he was found deep in the school's venting system, there was an alcohol container next to him.

He was found because he started to smell up the place.

When maintenance people investigated what they thought was a chemical leak, they found body parts and clothing.

It's cold in Alaska… some booze, a heating duct that emits carbon monoxide gas and reaches 300 degrees…

Why nobody ever hears, "Gee, I wish I had been drinking at the time."

21-YEAR-OLD DRUNK ASSAULTS WOMAN FOUR TIMES HIS AGE

A 21-year-old drunk told a judge he sexually assaulted an 82-year-old woman in an elevator.

The man put his hand over her mouth, tried to get her pants down and groped her.

Indeed, he must have been terribly drunk.

Man Killed For Stealing Two Bottles of Beer

The man "had previously stolen goods from my store, so I wanted to punish him," said the storekeeper as he looked down at his boots.

When the fellow came in and stole two bottles of beer, the 40-year-old store owner decided to kick and hit the punishment into him… till death did him part.

The dead guy, 50-60 years old, was found on the street unconscious* by a woman who was passing by. She called the police, who came and arrested the store owner on charges of "inflicting bodily injury resulting in death."

Gosh, you don't even have to be drunk to end up dead anymore.

*You are usually unconscious when you are dead.

FATHER AND SON PLAY TIC-TAC-TOE ON WOMAN'S BACK WITH A KNIFE

Two complete idiots raped and sexually assaulted a 41-year-old woman.

They then used a knife to play tic-tac-toe on her back.

The 45-year-old man and his 21-year-old poor excuse for a human being pleaded guilty.

The judge articulated, "the most appalling, degrading, humiliating and sadistic attack on a vulnerable woman in her own home… over a long period, without mercy, for thrills and for the joy of inflicting such humiliation, pain and distress on another human being."

The woman… met the guy in a bar… let him stay with her… then slept with him over an undisclosed period of time.

The offense… committed while the man and his son were drunk and on Ecstasy.

Is anyone surprised that booze was involved?

Tired of Being Stuck for Drinks? Woman Stabs Boyfriend–Sucks Blood

A fellow in AZ is bound to complain about being stuck for drinks.

His girlfriend tied him up, stabbed him and then drank his blood.

The woman said "I'm sorry. I didn't mean to hurt anyone."

Didn't mean to hurt anyone?!

Poking someone with a knife till enough blood comes out that it can be drunk is not likely to hurt someone?

Who's she kidding?

The tryst… alcohol- and drug-fueled…

Surprised that booze was involved?

Yeah, me, too.

Her lawyer: "she suffers from a personality disorder that causes instability and has taken responsibility for her actions."

Really, now. You don't say?

The woman thought she was a vampire for the first several weeks she was in jail.

Dang it, that doesn't shine any light on her mental state, now does it?

DRUNKEN TIFF LEADS TO GIRLFRIEND BEING STRANGLED

A 43-year-old man admitted to murdering his 40-year-old live-in girlfriend.

"We came home and got into a fight. I lost my temper and strangled her."

There's that Japanese efficiency... too much so.

The man called the police at around 6:10 p.m.

The argument started AFTER they came home drunk.

DRUNKEN DAD FAILS TO SEE BABY FALL OUT OF STROLLER

A drunken dad took his infant son for a walk in a stroller at 3 am.

He came back without the boy, NOT having noticed the little tike had fallen out.

I guess you can get pretty crazy driving a stroller drunk, too.

Another woman was awaken by the baby's cries. She found him in the dirt.

Pop had returned to the field to look for the baby.

"I could've sworn I had that baby with me when I was out here walking before."

The man will be charged with wanton endangerment.

I'd suggest we drop him in the field in the middle of the night and leave him there. But… then… he's probably already been there.

DRUNKEN MAN ALLOWS HIMSELF TO BE RUN OVER IN FRONT OF WIFE AND SON

A 44-year-old father and husband, drunk as a skunk, screamed, "I'm going to die," in front of his wife and 16-year-old son.

He then lay down in the street and two vehicles promptly ran over him and killed him while the missus and his son watched on.

The event took place at around 9:30 p.m.… causing us to wonder what ever happened to just passing out in a bar where you are relatively safe?

The son tried to pull his father to safety but couldn't do it in time.

Are there any dads reading this who drink? Can you feel the hurt of this son?

MOM SWINGS AND HITS BOYFRIEND WITH 4-WEEK-OLD BABY

Yup… sure enough. They had just come home from drinking… mom and her boyfriend.

A fight ensued and mom had all she could take.

So, she picked up her 4-week-old baby by the feet and swung him at her evil boyfriend and whacked him with the baby… cracking the baby's skull in the process.

She's facing five years mandatory minimum in the pokey. It's too short.

How about we pick the mother up and swing her by her feet and hit her head against the wall? Again… and again… and again…

Just how stupid can people be?

19-YEAR-OLD SHOT DEAD—HUNT STARTS IN BARS

A 19-year-old was shot dead at a New York subway station at 1:15 a.m.

The kid was shot in the head and pronounced dead at the scene.

Four or five men were seen fleeing the train station after the shooting.

The police started hunting for the culprits… in the bars and nightclubs.

When people do such stupid things, police will begin looking to see if they had been drinking or otherwise first.

LANE GARRISON OF PRISON BREAK TO DO REAL TIME

Lane Garrison of Prison Break fame will have to do real time... 40 months in jail for causing the death of a 17-year-old high school girl and injuring two other high-schoolers.

At the party, Garrison had a drink... took the three girls for a ride in his 2001 Land Rover.

A few minutes later he crossed over the median and hit a tree.

Garrison said he was sorry.

The girl is still dead.

His alcohol blood level... twice the legal limit for California.

Even Michael won't be able to get him out of this one.

Was it worth it, Lane?

JUDGE'S DRUNK DAUGHTER GUILTY IN FATAL WRECK

The 20-year-old daughter of a state district judge was driving an SUV with a blood alcohol level of .28, more than three times the legal limit of .08.

She slammed into the back of a box truck, killing her 19-year-old boyfriend.

The girl was 'like a daughter' to the family of her boyfriend, says the dead boy's father.

Now she can be the daughter …because they have no more son.

She got five years in jail that was probated to eight years. If she violates the probation… she goes to jail.

Enough?

6 HOURS OF DRINKING = 20 YEARS IN JAIL AND Y106 MILLION FINE

The driver, 28, and his passenger, 29, were ordered to pay Y106 million for driving and riding while drunk.

The car rammed into a group of high school students, killing three people and injuring 15 others.

The passenger was ordered to pay up as well because he spent 6 hours drinking with his buddy and asked the drunk to drive him home rather than sleep it off.

The car went through a red light and into the group of kids.

The driver also gets to spend 20 years in prison....

6 hours of drinking = 20 years in jail...

JAIL TIME AND JOB LOSS

I lost a brother and a sister to the 'drink'. My brother was on a motorbike, and my sister was driving her recliner… too drunk to walk out of the house when a fire started.

I have never heard anybody say, "Gee, I wish I had been drinking at the time."

Two reasons why drinking too much is stupid:

1. You can lose your job like this city government official in Japan.

After a round of drinks with friends, then another round and another, the idiot rode his motorbike home. Next thing he knew he woke up in a bed with a busted kneecap. "I don't remember where and what I drank."

2. You can end up in jail, the morgue or ALIVE.

It doesn't matter that you are Lindsay Lohan or anyone else for that matter. When the drink gets the best of you, the world sees your worst. Lohan must spend one night in jail, serve 36 months probation, complete an 18-month alcohol education program, pay her fines and complete a 3-day county coroner program where she must visit a morgue and talk to victims of drunken drivers.

If she screws up again… a mandatory 120-day jail sentence, unless friend Paris Hilton can give her some advice.

So, what's your excuse for not giving up booze?

2 Drunk Men and a Dead 9-Year-Old Girl

Two brothers, drunk and on drugs, raped a little 9-year-old girl in their dirty run-down camper, then strangled her because 'she looked up at him,' even though the little girl pleaded with them to stop.

One brother gets sick to his stomach when he hears a recounting of the story.

Well, wait till he sobers up, then let's see how he feels when he hears his sentencing.

TWO DRUNK TEENS MAKE "SHEET" GETAWAY - FALL 50 FEET

Two teenage girls, 14 years old, thought they could tie the sheets together and make a getaway by climbing down from the window before their parents caught them drinking.

Even adults would think they could do this if they were drunk enough.

The two girls went out the window and down 50 feet with a THUD resulting in broken bones and bruises and no hangover.

One of the parents found out they had been drinking and threatened to call the police... because of why? I wonder.

If a parent catches a kid drinking... where do the police come into the picture?

Well, if you are going to get caught drunk, you might as well break a bone or two to get some sympathy before punishment, eh?

Yeah, even adults would think like that when they get drunk.

GRIM REAPER BATTERS GIRL TO DEATH ON VALENTINE'S DAY

A 24-year-old boy, highly intelligent and oftentimes Grim Reaper, said he got a sexual thrill out of kicking and beating a 35-year-old care worker to death.

It was 'enjoyable and fun.'

The boy started binge-drinking when he went to university and became hooked.

Before killing his victim, a stranger to him, the boy had drunk at least five pints of lager before going to the club where he drank Carling, champagne, and Sambucca.

They spent two hours listening to country and western music at her apartment. When that didn't do the trick, he decided to take matters into his own hand.

He told police, "I actually quite enjoyed the experience; I remember thinking she was doing amazingly well not to be dead already."

He told police that he said, "I am monster. I am the grim reaper," as he stomped her to death… despite her pleading to placate him.

Still don't believe in the death penalty?

DRUNK JUMPS FROM SUV, DIES, IN FRONT OF HIS TWO KIDS

A 24-year-old man, drunk, jumped out of the SUV that was being driven by his 24-year-old wife with the couple's two children, 4 and 7 years old, in the back seat.

The man landed on the highway, northbound on Oregon 11, and died.

The car was going about 40-50 mph.

"Gee, dad… thanks for showing THAT to the kids."

KILL ME OR BE RAPED, INSISTS DRUNK DAD

A drunk stepdad dragged his 13-year-old stepdaughter out of bed and forced her into a chair.

"Either I rape you or you kill me."

He then cut his own wrists in front of her.

Miraculously, they did NOT let him just die.

Apparently when drunk, men can get their own miraculous powers—he beat his 15-year-old stepson and threw his wife out of the house and onto some concrete steps.

Steps… steps… steps…

The man has been sentenced to 14 months in jail.

That's it?

"Mom, can we have a say in who you marry next time? Please?"

CONCLUSION

The astute reader will notice the title says 101 Real Reasons Why You Never Hear Those Words, but that there are only 100 examples given.

Feeling cheated? Here are two more from my personal experience, giving you 101 and an extra.

My 42-year-old brother was drunk as a skunk, riding a newly-purchased motorbike. He misjudged a curb in the highway, drove into a grove of trees and didn't come back out alive.

Picture in your mind his 4-year-old son pacing the room asking, "Where's my daddy?"

"He's dead and not coming home."

"Mommy, what's dead?"

My 51-year-old sister was sitting at home, minding her own business, drinking in her chair and watching the tube, when her home caught on fire. Two steps from a sliding door and safety but too drunk to stand up and walk, she succumbed to the smoke and died in the fire.

Resolve to be different, to do things differently. To stop drinking completely if you don't know when to stop.

Change your life, starting now.

And, if you know somebody who needs to make a change, give them this book. It definitely can't hurt.

"'Gee, I wish I had been drinking at the time."

I have never heard anybody say those words. Have you?

Links

Readers who want to know the actual source of these stories can have their non-alcoholic search quenched by going to *www.wispid.com*

For those who want to know more about the illustrator, S.Akeala, also known as Benjamin Belew, please visit *www.sakeala.com*

And, for those who dare to read any more ramblings by the author, you will find plenty of material online at the following sites

www.billbelew.com – *my personal blog*
www.panasianbiz.com – *a blog about business in Asia*
www.thebizofknowledge.com – *about education and knowledge gained*
www.risingsunofnihon.com – *thoughts and notes about Japan*
www.greenpacks.org – *paperless writing about the environment*
www.theweeklydriver.com – *reviews of (some of them very nice) cars*
www.pacc.org – *my church's blog, to which I contribute*

ABOUT THE AUTHOR

Bill Belew is first a child, then an adult. He is a Christian, a child of God. He is an adult, the father of three amazing children: Benjamin (the illustrator for this book), Micah (US National champion swimmer) and Mia Mei ("M&M") who is young enough to be confused for being his granddaughter. Sometimes Bill gets so mad that just being mad isn't enough, he has to do something. For instance, there was the time he and his students redeemed some children in India who had been sold into slavery.

This book is another of a time when Bill hopes to make a difference in the world.

www.ingramcontent.com/pod-product-compliance
Lightning Source LLC
Chambersburg PA
CBHW020009050426
42450CB00005B/385